# Easter
## around the World

by Shannon Knudsen
illustrations by David L. Erickson

On My Own

HOLIDAYS

D0121881

**M** Millbrook Press/Minneapolis

*For peace-loving people around the world*
*—S.K.*

*To my two wonderful boys, and to their mother,*
*my wonderful wife*
*—D.L.E.*

Text copyright © 2005 by Carolrhoda Books, Inc.
Illustrations copyright © 2005 by David L. Erickson

*This book is available in two editions:*
Library binding by Millbrook Press, Inc., a division of Lerner Publishing Group
Soft cover by First Avenue Editions, an imprint of Lerner Publishing Group
241 First Avenue North
Minneapolis, MN 55401 U.S.A

Website address: www.lernerbooks.com


Library of Congress Cataloging-in-Publication Data

Knudsen, Shannon.
    Easter around the world / by Shannon Knudsen ; illustrations by
David L. Erickson.
        p.   cm. — (On my own holidays)
    Contents: What is Easter? — Sweden — Ethiopia — Russia —
Egypt — Mexico — Philippines — Colombia — Germany.
    ISBN-13: 978–1–57505–655–5 (lib. bdg. : alk. paper)
    ISBN-10: 1–57505–655–0 (lib. bdg. : alk. paper)
    ISBN-13: 978–1–57505–765–1 (pbk. : alk. paper)
    ISBN-10: 1–57505–765–4 (pbk. : alk. paper)
    1. Easter — Juvenile literature. [1. Easter.]  I. Erickson, David L., ill.
II. Title. III. Series.
GT4935.Z45 2005
394.2667                                                    2003023420

Manufactured in the United States of America
3  4  5  6  7  8  –  DP  –  12  11  10  09  08  07

# Table of Contents

# What Is Easter?

Easter is a holiday that usually takes place on a Sunday in March or April. In some countries, it is also celebrated in May. For people who follow the Christian religion, Easter is one of the most important holidays of the year.

Christians believe that Jesus is the son of God. They also believe that Jesus died and came back to life. Easter is remembered as the day that Jesus came back to life.

The word *Easter* probably comes from a very old word that means "spring." Easter takes place in the spring in many parts of the world. After a long, cold winter, Easter is a time to welcome the new life and growth that springtime brings. Many people who are not Christians celebrate Easter for this reason.

People around the world mark Easter in different ways. Some Easter traditions are shared by many cultures. Other traditions are followed by people in just one area. For those who join in this special holiday, Easter is a day for feasting, spending time with family, and celebrating new life.

# Sweden

DINGDONG! DINGDONG!

Doorbells ring all over Sweden on the
Thursday and Saturday before Easter.
Who is at the door?
Witches!
These Easter witches are really
just girls in costumes.

Old Swedish stories tell how
the week before Easter is a time
when witches gather.
That's why girls dress as witches then.
Sometimes boys dress up, too.

The little witches wear their mothers'
skirts, aprons, and head scarves.
They use makeup to paint
red circles on their cheeks.
Some children carry broomsticks.
The witches go from door to door.
They call out Easter greetings
to their neighbors.
Each witch holds up a copper
kettle or a coffeepot,
hoping for a gift of candy or money.

Swedish families eat Easter dinner
on the Saturday night before Easter.
They feast on fish, ham, lamb,
and boiled Easter eggs.

Then the children hunt for eggs
that their parents have hidden.
One egg is hidden for each child.
This egg isn't a real egg.
It's made of colored cardboard,
and it's packed full of delicious candy.

11

# Ethiopia

On the night before Easter,
Ethiopian Christians fill their churches.
People pray and sing for hours.
After church, everyone goes home to eat.

People bring gifts of food
to their friends and family.
The Easter feast lasts
for two days or more.
It often includes mutton,
the meat of a sheep.
Some families read the Bible
as part of their celebration.

Many people play a game called *gebeta*.
Gebeta is a board game played with pieces,
like checkers or chess.
Seeds, stones, or beans are used
for gebeta pieces.
The board is carved from wood.
It has cups cut into the wood.
Each player moves pieces
from cup to cup, trying to
capture the other player's pieces.
The player who captures
all the pieces wins.

# Russia

The week before Easter brings
many chores for Russian families.
Everyone wants to have a clean
house for Easter dinner.
Children help their parents
dust, sweep, and mop.
Some people even paint their walls
so that they look clean and new.
Between chores, families shop
for new Easter clothes.

Many families go to church
on the night before Easter.
The service ends in the
middle of the night.
But it isn't bedtime.
It's time for the Easter feast!
The main dish is roasted meat.
There are plenty of Easter eggs, too.
Dessert is a sweet, creamy
cheese called *pashka*.
Pashka is covered with
nuts and dried fruit.
It tastes delicious with an
Easter cake called *kulich*.
Kulich is baked in a can
so that it stands tall.
It's filled with fruit and nuts
and covered with sweet icing.

Easter celebrations go on for
the rest of the week.
When people meet, they give
each other three kisses
and an Easter greeting.

Children play a game
with their Easter eggs.
Each player taps an egg
against another player's egg.
The person whose egg breaks first
must give it to the other player.

Some of the world's most famous
Easter eggs came from Russia.
They were made by a jeweler
named Peter Carl Fabergé.
Starting in 1885, he made beautiful eggs
every Easter for the rulers of Russia.
Fabergé used gold, silver, and other
precious metals to create his eggs.
He covered each egg with dazzling gems.
Most of his eggs opened up
to reveal a surprise.
One egg held a gold ship.
Another held an eagle made of diamonds.
Fabergé eggs are known as works
of art all over the world.

# Egypt

Easter is a joyful day
for Christians in Egypt.
People go to church in the morning.
Then they gather with their families
for an Easter feast.
They eat turkey, lamb, and grape leaves
stuffed with meat and rice.
Many children receive gifts
of new clothes from their parents.
Sometimes children are given money, too.

For fun, Egyptian children
have egg-rolling contests.
Each child sends an Easter egg
rolling down a hill.
The egg that reaches the bottom
first is the winner.

# Mexico

Easter starts early in Mexico.
During the week before Easter Sunday,
people march in many parades.
The marchers wear costumes
and act out the story
of the last days of Jesus's life.

After the parades,
a play called the Passion Play
tells the story of how Jesus died.
In Mexico City, thousands of people
take part in the Passion Play.
Millions of people come to watch.

Many people go to church
on the night before Easter.
Then they gather in the town square.
Men hang up colorful paper figures.
Some figures stand for enemies
of the Mexican people.
One figure stands for the devil.
BANG!
Suddenly, firecrackers explode.
The paper figures blow up.
They fall to the ground in tiny pieces.
The crowd cheers.

On Easter morning,
church bells ring out loudly.
People go to church.
Afterward, the town square fills
again with happy families.
Parents buy ice cream, snow cones,
and balloons for their children.
Some towns even have
carnival rides to add to the fun.

30

# Philippines

Easter in the Philippines begins
as the sun rises.
Girls dress up as angels.
Their mothers take them to
one end of their town.

The women and girls bring a statue
of Mary, the mother of Jesus.
The statue's face is covered
with a black veil.
The veil is a sign of Mary's sadness
because Jesus has died.

Boys and men go to the
other end of the town.
They carry a statue of Jesus.
The two groups march in a parade
toward the center of town.
When they meet, they place the statues of
Mary and Jesus next to each other.
The children sing an Easter song.

One of the girls removes Mary's veil.

Under the veil, Mary's face is smiling.

She is happy to see that her son

has risen from the dead.

White doves are released

from cages as a sign of peace.

Then the families go to church together

to celebrate the holiday.

# Colombia

NEIGH! NEIGH!

The burros of San Antero have a lot to say

on the day before Easter.

*Burro* is Spanish for donkey.

Most of the year, burros work hard

pulling carts and plows.

But on this day, they are the stars

of a beauty contest!

Farm families do their best to make their burros look perfect for the contest.
Every burro has a costume.
Male burros wear suits and ties.
Female burros wear dresses and hats.
Some wear bathing suits!

Everyone in town comes
to watch the contest.
The most beautiful male and
female burros win.
What is their prize?
It is one that any burro would like.
The beautiful burros
never have to work again!

# Germany

German homes are full of bright
decorations for Easter.
Many people bring home yellow
daffodils and pink cherry blossoms.
The flowers remind everyone
that spring has come.
Some families bring willow branches
inside and put them in a vase.
Easter eggs are hung on the branches
to make an egg tree.

In some parts of Germany,
Easter treats are brought by a fox,
a crane, or a cuckoo bird.
But in most places, children hope
for a visit from the Easter Hare.
On the day before Easter, children
build little nests of twigs and straw.
They hope the Easter Hare will
lay eggs in the nests during the night.

Some children also make a
special Easter egg for their parents.
On this egg, they write a
promise to do chores.

Early on Easter morning,

the children run to check the nests

they made the day before.

They find chocolate bunnies,

chocolate eggs, and colorful Easter eggs.

After eating their sweet treats,

the children have egg hunts and games.

They give their special eggs to

their parents, too.

Then many families go to church.

They spend the rest of Easter

enjoying a good meal

and visiting their loved ones.

Together they share the joy

that Easter and springtime bring.

# Easter Nests

*For a new Easter treat, try making these tiny nests filled with colorful Easter eggs. Ask an adult to help.*

You will need:

**1 cup butterscotch chips**

**½ cup peanut butter**

**2 cups chow mein noodles**

**1 tablespoon butter (for buttering fingers)**

**jelly beans**

1. Put butterscotch chips and peanut butter in a microwave-safe bowl. Heat on medium power for 3 minutes. Use a pot holder to remove bowl. Stir mixture.
2. If mixture is not completely melted, heat again on medium for 1 minute. Stir and repeat until mixture is completely melted.
3. Add chow mein noodles. Stir until mixture covers noodles.
4. Butter fingers. Place handfuls of mixture on waxed paper and shape into nests.
5. Let cool. Fill nests with jelly beans.
   Makes about 6 nests.